# How to Play Lacrosse for Beginners

*The Ultimate Guide to Mastering Everything from Rules, Equipment, Sticks, and Etiquette to Ball Control, Shooting, and Defending*

© **Copyright 2023 - All rights reserved.**

The content contained within this book may not be reproduced, duplicated, or transmitted without direct written permission from the author or the publisher.

Under no circumstances will any blame or legal responsibility be held against the publisher, or author, for any damages, reparation, or monetary loss due to the information contained within this book, either directly or indirectly.

**Legal Notice:**

This book is copyright protected. It is only for personal use. You cannot amend, distribute, sell, use, quote, or paraphrase any part of the content within this book without the consent of the author or publisher.

**Disclaimer Notice:**

Please note the information contained within this document is for educational and entertainment purposes only. All effort has been executed to present accurate, up-to-date, reliable, and complete information. No warranties of any kind are declared or implied. Readers acknowledge that the author is not engaging in the rendering of legal, financial, medical, or professional advice. The content within this book has been derived from various sources. Please consult a licensed professional before attempting any techniques outlined in this book.

By reading this document, the reader agrees that under no circumstances is the author responsible for any losses, direct or indirect, that are incurred as a result of the use of the information contained within this document, including, but not limited to, errors, omissions, or inaccuracies.

# Table of Contents

Introduction —————————————————————————— 1

Chapter 1: Getting Started ————————————————— 3

Chapter 2: Lacrosse Equipment ——————————————— 14

Chapter 3: Lacrosse Sticks and Ball———————————— 23

Chapter 4: Lacrosse Positions and
Team Play ————————————————————————— 30

Chapter 5: Ball Control and Passing ———————————— 42

Chapter 6: Shooting and Scoring ——————————————— 55

Chapter 7: Lacrosse Defense ————————————————— 66

Chapter 8: Improving Your Game and
Lacrosse Community————————————————————— 77

Conclusion ————————————————————————— 85

References ————————————————————————— 87

# Introduction

Lacrosse is taking the world by storm, with more players and fans flocking to the field than ever before. If you've witnessed the thrill of a lacrosse game or had the opportunity to play or coach this sport, you already understand its magnetic appeal. In this book, you'll learn the very essence of lacrosse's remarkable rise in popularity and why it has become a favorite among enthusiasts.

At its core, lacrosse is a unique blend of various sports, making it an exciting and accessible sport for people of all shapes and sizes. It incorporates the rugged physicality of football, the lightning-fast pace of hockey, and basketball's strategic passing and transitions. Virtually anyone can pick up a lacrosse stick and join the game, whether you're on the smaller side with speed and agility or larger and more robust. Once you venture into the world of lacrosse, you'll quickly realize it's a game that gets under your skin and refuses to let go. It's simply habit-forming.

In the following pages, you'll travel through lacrosse's intriguing aspects, breaking down the fundamentals, rules, and strategies to set you on the path to becoming a confident player or a knowledgeable coach. Whether you're completely new to the sport or have prior experience, this guide will help you grasp the beauty and excitement of lacrosse and equip you with the skills and understanding to jump into action confidently.

So, if you're ready to unlock the exhilarating world of lacrosse, dive in and discover the joy, passion, and endless possibilities this sport has to offer. Welcome to the beginner's guide to playing lacrosse.

# Chapter 1: Getting Started

Lacrosse is more popular than ever for a few simple reasons. More people in more places are being introduced to the sport. It's easy to get hooked once you watch it because it's a mix of exciting elements from popular sports like football, basketball, and hockey. It's fast-paced, challenging, and never boring. The great thing is you don't have to be super strong or big to do well in lacrosse.

In this chapter, you'll learn the basics of lacrosse, the game rules, etiquette, and the distinctions between men's and women's games. So, whether you're trying lacrosse for the first time, aiming to improve your skills, or a parent or fan, there's something in this book for you. This chapter is only the beginning of your journey into the exciting world of lacrosse.

# Lacrosse Basics

1. *Watching lacrosse can be overwhelming. Source: https://unsplash.com/photos/lacrosse-players-on-sports-field-LrTk9HYK2po?utm_content=creditShareLink&utm_medium=referral&utm_source=unsplash*

If you're watching a lacrosse game for the first time, it can be a bit overwhelming. There's a lot happening on the field. Players are constantly running on and off the field, the possession of the ball can change quickly, and there are a lot of physical hits, except in women's lacrosse, where contact is limited.

Lacrosse is a game that involves a lot of running, dodging, spinning, cutting, and faking. It's full of excitement, from players sprinting on a fast break to outmaneuvering opponents to score a goal.

One thing that makes lacrosse exciting is it's a high-scoring game. If you ever see a game where no goals are scored (a shutout), it's a rare event because it's not something you'll see often.

In lacrosse, the key is to throw the ball accurately, but the unique part is that you use a stick to do it, not your hands. The ball in lacrosse is about 8 inches in circumference and 2½ inches in diameter, weighing a bit over 5 ounces.

While it may not be easy, with good coaching and practice, almost anyone can quickly learn the basic skills to play. Unlike many other team sports where size and strength are crucial, lacrosse is a sport that also rewards those who are small and speedy. Being big helps, especially if you're fast, but smaller players can excel in lacrosse if they are quick, smart, aggressive, and skilled with a lacrosse stick.

## The Rules

Lacrosse is a team sport played between two teams, each consisting of a minimum of 10 players. These players are traditionally categorized into four main positions: attackers, midfielders, defense, and goalie. While some teams may introduce specialty positions, these four roles are the most universally used.

1. **Attackers**

   These players are the primary offensive force on the team. Their role is to score goals, but their responsibilities extend beyond this. In instances where a shot doesn't result in a goal, attackers must strive to regain possession of the ball and prevent the opposing defense from clearing it. They must always be alert to the ball's location to avoid losing possession.

## 2. Defense

Defenders have one of the most challenging roles on the field. Their primary responsibility is to thwart the opposing team's attempts to score. Most defenders use sticks with longer handles, allowing them to cover a larger field area. Playing defense is a demanding and sometimes perilous role, as defenders can find themselves in the line of fire when the opposing team takes shots at goal. Awareness of their surroundings and the ball's location is crucial to proper defensive play.

## 3. Midfielders

Midfielders are versatile players who engage in the offensive and defensive aspects of the game. They need strong offensive skills and the ability to swiftly transition to defense when required. Midfielders with exceptional stamina are the most well-rounded athletes on the team. Even though they only spend short periods on the field, they must perform at full speed during every second when on it.

## 4. Goalie

The goalie's role is straightforward: to prevent shots from entering the net. However, their responsibilities go beyond stopping shots. Goalies are responsible for clearing the ball after making a save and communicating with their teammates throughout the opponent's possession.

Field lacrosse fields can have varying dimensions based on the competition level. For high school and beyond, the field measures 110 yards in length and 60 yards in width. In youth lacrosse, the field dimensions can vary significantly due to space constraints and making the game accessible for beginners. The field is marked by several key lines and areas:

**1. Center Line**

This divides the field into two halves - the defensive and offensive sides. Players are mandated to maintain a specific number on each side, a rule akin to ice hockey. Face-offs are initiated at the midpoint of this center line.

**2. Goal Line Extended**

These are imaginary lines extending from the goal line to the sidelines. Both offensive and defensive teams use this line, with defenders staying on the top side of this line to prevent attackers from advancing beyond it.

**3. End Line**

The end line marks the rear boundary of the playing field.

The field is further divided into various playing zones:

**4. Wing Area**

These areas are parallel to the sideline and located 20 yards from the face-off X on both sides of the field. During face-offs, wingers line up behind this line, and it extends 10 yards in both directions from the midline. One winger usually takes an offensive position, while the other assumes a defensive stance.

**5. Offensive Area**

This area is delineated by a solid line positioned 20 yards above the goal line extended. It extends 20 yards in both directions from the center of the field and further extends to the back-end line, running parallel to the sidelines. The offensive area measures 40 yards in width and 35 yards in depth.

### 6. Defensive Area

This is the mirror image of the offensive area, located on the defensive half of the field. Passing lanes and strategies are significant in this area. Defensive and offensive players use these lanes, and the ball moves through these areas. Defenses also use the top of the box as a reference for picking up and applying pressure. When teams employ zone defenses, they use the top of the box to identify the seams in the zone. These lines are critical for offensive and defensive teams when executing their riding and clearing patterns.

## Forms of Lacrosse

Lacrosse has two main forms: Field Lacrosse and Box Lacrosse.

### 1. Field Lacrosse

This version is more popular in the United States and originated with Native Americans. The number of players on the field varies depending on whether it's the men's or women's game. The field is 110 yards long and 60 yards wide for men and slightly larger for women. The goals are 6 feet high and 6 feet wide.

### 2. Box Lacrosse

Box lacrosse is more popular in Canada and is played on a surface similar to an ice hockey rink but with artificial turf instead of ice. Unlike field lacrosse, box lacrosse has fewer players, only 6 on each team. These players have different roles based on their positions, like offense, transition, or defense. The playing surface is smaller, about 180 to 200 feet long and 80 to 90 feet wide. The goals are also smaller, measuring 4 feet in height and 4 feet in width. Goalies in box lacrosse wear more protective gear, and the game usually has more scoring than field lacrosse.

## Fouls and Game Etiquette

Different fouls are penalized in lacrosse and can be broadly categorized into two groups: Personal Fouls and Technical Fouls. Here's an in-depth look at both:

**Personal Fouls**

Personal fouls are more severe infractions and can lead to a player's suspension from the game for 1 to 3 minutes, depending on the foul's severity and intent. The ball is awarded to the opposing team, creating an extra-man opportunity for the fouled team. The fouling team plays with fewer players for the duration of the penalty.

1. **Slashing**

    This is one of the most frequently called fouls. It results from a player's uncontrolled check, which misses its intended target (usually the opponent's glove or stick) and contacts the body or head of the ball carrier. Even a stick check that hits the arm or body of the offensive player can be considered a slash. The judgment of whether a legal check turned into a slash is up to the official.

2. **Tripping**

Tripping occurs when a player uses a body part or stick to trip an opponent, often unintentionally, when competing for a loose ball.

3. **Illegal Body Check**

Although body checking is legal, it's rarely allowed due to the likelihood of various infractions, such as hitting above the shoulders, following through with the shaft of the stick, or applying unnecessary roughness. It should mainly be used when a player makes the second-slide attempt to stop the offensive player from penetrating the defense, similar to taking charge in basketball.

4. **Cross-Checking**

This foul happens when a player checks, holds or pushes an opponent in the back or side with the shaft of their stick. It's illegal to check an opponent with the handle of a stick held between both hands.

5. **Unnecessary Roughness**

Unnecessary roughness is called when an infraction of the rules, such as holding, pushing, or hitting, is excessively violent. It also includes deliberately running into a player, setting a pick with violent intent.

6. **Unsportsmanlike Conduct**

A team member can assess unsportsmanlike conduct or anyone officially associated with the team for various infractions, such as arguing excessively with an official's call, using threatening or obscene language or gestures, or repeatedly committing the same technical foul. It can also be called when a player deliberately fails to comply with the rules for entering the field of play. A player who accumulates five personal fouls will be disqualified from the game.

A player or team member can be removed from the game for fighting, leaving the bench during an altercation, using tobacco, committing a second non-releasable unsportsmanlike penalty, or for misconduct deemed by the officials. Regardless of goals scored, a non-releasable penalty must be served for the entire duration.

**Technical Fouls**

Technical fouls are less severe than personal fouls and lead to a 30-second penalty or a loss of possession if the fouling team had the ball at the time of the foul. The ball is given to the other team where the foul occurred.

1. **Holding**

   This penalty is called when a player impedes the movement of the opponent's stick. The defensive player cannot use their stick to hold an opponent or check an opponent's stick without the ball.

2. **Offside**

   Offside is called when a team has more players on the offensive or defensive half of the field than allowed. Teams are limited to four players on the defensive and three on the offensive half, regardless of their positions.

3. **Interference**

   A player should not interfere with the free movement of an opponent unless they are the ball carrier or within 5 yards of the ball. This rule protects the offensive player.

### 4. Illegal Offensive Screening (Setting Picks)

Offensive players cannot move into or make contact with a defensive player, denying them access to the player they are guarding. Offensive players must remain motionless when setting screens.

### 5. Crease Violations

Interfering with the goalie in the crease, even if he doesn't have possession, is a play-on situation. The crease area is the space used by the goalie, and a play-on is when the goalie has possession and is allowed to run the ball out of the crease. If the ball is loose in the crease, and the goalie gets possession after the play-on signal, the defensive team regains possession at the midfield X position.

### 6. Stalling

Teams are given 10 seconds from bringing the ball over the midline to get it into the offensive zone. During the last 2 minutes of regulation play, stalling rules are in effect for the team ahead.

### 7. Illegal Procedure

This covers a range of actions that do not conform to the rules, such as touching the ball, interfering with an opponent's stick, or violating substitution rules.

These personal or technical fouls play a significant role in the game and require players and officials to make quick decisions and maintain a fair and safe playing environment.

Lacrosse is a fast and intense game where many things are happening all at once. You must keep an eye on offense, defense, special teams, and the goalie simultaneously. It's like juggling multiple balls in the air. To be good at lacrosse, you must be able to handle all these different aspects of the game and switch between them quickly during the game. The game doesn't slow down, so you must stay focused and be ready for anything.

# Chapter 2: Lacrosse Equipment

Lacrosse is a full-impact, high-octane sport, so quality equipment that meets safety standards is essential. Since lacrosse is a team sport, each position functions differently, requiring players to have specialized equipment catered to their job on the field. Therefore, before purchasing any gear, you need to know the role you will fulfill. Also, there are some differences between women's and men's lacrosse, so gender-specific gear must be considered. Knowing precisely what you need as a beginner prevents you from wandering around, uncertain of what to purchase from the array of equipment available.

Lacrosse is a technical sport, so there are variations of equipment for different ages and skill levels. This chapter explores the wide range of equipment available on the market and provides a detailed description to determine what will work best for you. The gear can be divided into two essential parts: equipment like the stick, ball, and goal posts, and safety gear, like your helmet and shoulder pads. Get ready to lace up your cleats and discover the fast-paced magic of lacrosse.

# Essential Gear for Lacrosse Players

Lacrosse teams are divided into four basic positions: defenders, attackers, midfielders, and goalie. Each position has specialized equipment to improve their performance on the field and keep them safe in this full-contact sport. Men's and women's lacrosse differ slightly, so the gear also varies. Women's lacrosse is less aggressive than their male counterparts, so comparatively, the equipment is minimal. The basics for the women's game are a stick, a mouthguard, and protective goggles to prevent eye injuries. Some players wear headgear and protective gloves, but this is not required except for the goalie, who is mandated to wear a face-protecting helmet, a throat protector, a chest protector, and thick padded gloves to prevent your hands' fragile bones from getting shattered.

Safety is a greater concern in the men's game because there is more head-on clashing and confrontational physicality. Unlike their female counterparts, all male players are required to wear headgear. Players of both genders use a ball, a stick, and six-foot-high goalposts. The additional protection men have are shoulder pads, arm guards, and a cup to protect the sensitive groin area. Gear must meet the standards of various sports organizations, like the Safety Equipment Institute and The National Operating Committee on Standards for Athletic Equipment. Counterfeit gear that has not undergone strenuous testing to be certified is available on the market, so be vigilant. The standards have been developed to protect you while you compete and have fun. Goalies usually have the most safety gear because the ball is constantly hurled at them at unimaginable speeds. Therefore, if you are in the posts, you need a chest protector, throat guard, and facemask.

Since every player has a specialized duty like defending, attacking, or, in the case of midfielders, switching between these roles, different sticks are more suited for particular functions. The shafts on midfielders' and attackers' sticks are typically shorter, ranging from 40 to 42 inches. Sometimes, midfielders are used as defensive support. This supporting role is known as a long-stick midfielder because they will carry a stick like those of defensive players rather than attackers. Defenders and long stick midfielders use a shaft ranging from 52 to 60 inches. The "head" is the part on the end of the stick that holds the ball. The width and length of the head will determine how easy or difficult it is to control the ball. Size and age specifications determine the head's size appropriate for competition. The string forming the pocket on the head is called meshing. Specific rules for meshing depend on the league, skill levels, and age groups.

Besides the stick, the ball is probably the most important piece of equipment because there is no game without it. Lacrosse balls are made from a rubbery material in a range of colors but are usually white in men's games and yellow for women. Many different balls are used for different games, like training exercises or indoor play. The ball's look, texture, and weight can change according to its purpose. People use these different balls for training and developing various skill sets. The balls used professionally are standardized and must comply with internal guidelines.

# Selecting the Right Lacrosse Stick

2. *Comfort is important when choosing a lacrosse stick. Source: Henning Schlottmann (User:H-stt), CC BY-SA 4.0 <https://creativecommons.org/licenses/by-sa/4.0>, via Wikimedia Commons: https://commons.wikimedia.org/wiki/File:Lacrosse_stick_8026.jpg*

Your comfort is one of the central factors when choosing the right lacrosse stick. What works perfectly for one player may be terrible for your game. As a beginner, experimenting with a few different sticks is advisable. If possible, first borrow some sticks from your team or an individual so that you can get a feel of what works best. Your height, age, and skill level will determine which stick suits you best.

Attackers and midfielders use shorter sticks because it increases their ability to control the ball, and better able to scoop up ground balls and hold onto the ball securely, preventing the opposition from getting it. Therefore, if you are interested in playing an attacking role, you will need a short stick. According to the rules, the defensive stick size can be as short as 52 inches up to 72 inches. The goalie's stick is a medium length, between attackers' and defenders' sizes. Their stick can range from 40 inches to 72 inches, so they have a lot of wiggle room to work with. Some goalies prefer shorter sticks because they increase their reaction time, while others choose a longer stick so they can clear and pass the ball across large distances on the field more accurately.

Besides the stick's length, other factors contribute to maximizing your skill and comfort level in the game. Players have preferences when it comes to the weight and feel of the stick. In the past, lacrosse sticks were mostly made from wood, but today, numerous materials are used, each with its own pros and cons. Younger or smaller players favor aluminum sticks because of their lightweight. These sticks are great for beginners but are not durable and do not accommodate advanced grips. Alloy sticks are the perfect replacement for aluminum sticks because they are also stronger and lightweight. Offensive players favor them, and they are a beginner's dream, being both strong and affordable. Scandium shafts are fast becoming the professional standard because they are also lightweight and strong. These sticks can be used in any position but are quite pricey and more suited for elite players. Manufacturers are developing blended sticks by combining materials. These sticks are scientifically crafted to produce the best strength-to-weight ratios. They are versatile and can be used in many positions.

As a beginner, do not break the bank to buy your first stick. You are still learning and getting used to the game and will develop preferences as you progress. Buy a light, durable stick that costs you $20 to $60. For intermediate and professional players, more professional sticks can shoot up to $150. More advanced players buy their shafts and heads separately and often customize their grips. You can only learn what combination is best with experience in the field. Once players develop a playing style, they can adjust their stick to match. As a beginner, you want a stick versatile enough to adjust on the field and strong enough to endure rookie mistakes when learning the game.

## Protective Gear

Your safety equipment must fit properly to work effectively. Your head is the control tower of the body, and a severe head injury can drastically change your life. The size of your helmet is also crucial, so make sure the gear fits snuggly on your head. Your helmet's chin strap must be firmly secured, and the headgear should not have any slack, allowing it to move around. If you had long, thick hair when you fitted a helmet and later cut it, it may be necessary to resize the equipment. Besides the goalie, the participants do not usually wear headgear in women's lacrosse. However, they are still required to wear goggles, which should also fit well and not move while ensuring their vision is not impaired.

3. *Your safety equipment must fit properly to work effectively. Source: https://www.pexels.com/photo/man-holding-white-lacrosse-stick-standing-on-green-grass-field-during-daytime-159564/*

Footwear is an integral part of safety equipment that is easy to overlook. The cleats you purchase must fit your foot well and be comfortable. Cleats provide the grip to prevent slipping when making the explosive movements necessary to play lacrosse well. You will feel the difference if you play with regular running shoes or sneakers. Losing grip while running and turning at full speed can cause irreversible ankle and knee injuries, so you must prevent these serious injuries. Spending a decent chunk on a quality brand will benefit in the long term because they last longer and are more comfortable than cheaper brands. Lacrosse requires constant running, so what you have on your feet will massively impact your game.

The full-contact nature of lacrosse requires chest and rib protection. The rules allow players to body-check one another, which could be devastating at a fast pace without proper covering. The stick presents an additional element of danger even though it is prohibited to hit players with it. Mistakes happen, so your body protection also serves the purpose of guardian against injuries caused by the stick. In addition to chest and rib guards, arm and elbow protection is crucial to reduce harm. Injuries in a full-contact sport are almost unavoidable, but you can use safety measures that mitigate excessive harm. The groin is a very sensitive area, and injury can have dire consequences, so do not forget to wear a cup before setting foot on the field. Shin pads are also worn because legs can make contact in the heat of the game.

The goalie comes into contact with a high-speed ball flung directly at their face. Hence, a goalkeeper needs additional protection, like throat guards. A knock from a rubber ball zipping through the air can cut off your airway so severely that it can be life-threatening. It can be tempting to fool around on the field without safety gear for some light fun, but the danger is not worth it for a few good-time giggles. Safety equipment allows lacrosse to be playable without an increased risk of devastating consequences. Safety should come first whether you are outfield or in the posts as a goalkeeper.

Lacrosse players wear the same mouthguards as hockey players. These guards protect your teeth and help reduce the likelihood of concussions. When you are hit hard enough, your teeth rattle, causing your brain to shake. The trauma the brain suffers from getting shaken is what causes concussions. Mouth guards prevent your teeth from rattling, significantly reducing the severity of concussions. Furthermore, they protect your teeth, so you can keep your gorgeous smile while enjoying one of the most high-speed, full-impact sports.

# Chapter 3: Lacrosse Sticks and Ball

The ball and stick are the central pieces of the game. It is impossible to play lacrosse without a ball, stick, and goalposts. Understanding sticks and ball varieties available on the market and how they are used in different scenarios will greatly improve your game. These key elements of the game require a firm grasp of how the stick and ball function, from cradling, where a player rocks their stick back and forth while running with the ball, to passing, clearing, and shooting.

    Knowing why a stick is shaped the way it is and the significance of different weights and lengths will give insight into how to manipulate the ball in your favor during games. Lacrosse plays are built by getting players into the right scoring and defending positions so that they can use their bodies and sticks strategically. The small details of how the stick is designed may seem trivial, but understanding your utensils makes you a better chef so you can cook up heat on the field. It is nearly impossible to play lacrosse without the right equipment, unlike some sports that do not require much. There is no authentic way to set up a make-shift lacrosse game because it will endanger the players if the correct equipment is not used.

Different lacrosse balls react in unique ways. The bounce and how the ball rolls or flies will adjust how you handle the ball. Although professional leagues have standardized balls, you will find different balls when playing at an amateur level when you compete. Having a basic familiarity with how different balls can be used mindfully to ensure victory gives you an undeniable edge, especially as a beginner. As you start playing, you will tangibly experience how proper use of your stick can change the outcome of games because varying skills in controlling the ball can swing matches at pivotal moments.

## Types of Lacrosse Sticks

As a beginner, it can be tempting just to jump in and buy the first stick the salesperson at your local sports shop suggests. However, much more consideration goes into buying the right stick. You will probably use the same stick for more than a year, and if you play consistently, it means you spend a lot of time with this tool. Since sticks are not often bought, you want to make sure you get the perfect match. Therefore, understanding the sticks available on the market and their uses is essential to making a buying decision you will not regret. The more informed you are about sticks, the less likely you will use equipment that adversely impacts you in games, reducing much-needed advantages.

A lacrosse stick comprises three parts: the head, the shaft, and the mesh. The head is the bucket-shaped plastic part on the end of the stick which makes contact with the ball. You cannot use your hands or feet to manipulate the ball in lacrosse, so the head is crucial to gameplay because it is the part that will touch the ball most often. The head is divided into sections, including the scoop and the side wall. The scoop is the rounded tip wider than the rest of the head. This scoop is used to pick the ball up from the ground. The sidewall is where the mesh of the netting is weaved through.

4. *The head is the bucket-shaped part on the end of the stick. Source: Raffi Basralian, Public domain, via Wikimedia Commons: https://commons.wikimedia.org/wiki/File:Lacrosse_stick_head.jpg*

The shaft is the extended section of the stick the player grips. Your shaft will be longer or shorter, depending on your position. Defenders need long sticks, attackers use short sticks, and midfielders vary between the two. The mesh is the netting used to cradle the ball. The mesh is often made from nylon and varies in hardness. Some players prefer softer mesh, and others prefer harder mesh. Soft mesh is best for a beginner because it is easier to string. Many types of mesh are available on the market, and each has a slightly varying influence on the game.

Another more beautiful sounding and formal name for a lacrosse stick is the crosse. Players can customize their sticks, but they must fall within the regulatory outlines of the rules. Therefore, there are limits on how long or short your stick can be. Sticks are sometimes cut to match the height of shorter players in youth leagues. But from high school and beyond, this practice is usually uncommon. Examples of stick specifications mandated by the rules are that the scoop cannot be wider than 6.5 inches and the head cannot be longer than 10 inches. These rules ensure players do not have unfair advantages when handling the ball.

The lacrosse sticks' shafts must be comfortable because this is the section players hold onto throughout the game. Shafts can be shaped differently depending on the player's comfort. They can be rounder or hexagonal. When you lay it flat on the ground, the head is slightly angled upwards on the shaft. Shafts can be plastic, wood, or a combination of other materials. Most shafts in the modern game are typically made by combining different materials to achieve the best strength, weight, and durability. Classic lacrosse shafts were made completely from wood, but this approach changed as technology advanced.

As the size of the stick varies between attackers and defenders, the goalkeeper also has a specialized stick. Out of all the players on the field, the goalkeeper has the most distinctive stick because of the role's requirements. The stick is 52 inches long, but the head is much wider than other sticks on the field because it is meant to catch the ball to block it from going into the net. The goalie stays in their crease and does not venture out onto the field.

Before you purchase a stick, you must know what kind of player you are, what you are comfortable with, your style of play, and the skills or attributes you want to maximize. Alloy sticks, made from a mixture of different metals, are excellent for entry-level players because they are so easy to use. Composite shafts are more flexible and have a specialized engraved grip. The flex on these shafts allows players to shoot with more aggressive speed, so they are typically used by attacking players. Manufacturers are developing sticks that are a blend of alloy, scandium, and other materials. The versatility of these sticks makes them the perfect fit for midfielders because they will perform defending and attacking duties.

As a beginner, you may want to hold off on buying a stick until you've played the game. Many teams provide players with equipment, or you can borrow a stick. Once you get the hang of the sport, know which position you'll play, and the stick best catering to your game, you can make the expensive commitment of buying a quality stick. The options on the market are endless, and manufacturers provide detailed descriptions of their products. Before committing to a stick, conduct thorough research, read reviews, and test as many sticks as possible.

## Understanding Lacrosse Balls

Depending on your league and its rules, lacrosse balls will have different specifications, like weight, shape, material, and color. The ball's color is important because it can increase or reduce visibility. Playing lacrosse with a green ball is not advisable because it will blend in with the grass. The most common ball color is white, but fluorescent neon colors are also used. Teams typically use different colored balls for matches and practice. For goalie training, a ball with high visibility is preferable because they can work on focusing their eyes and building their reflexes. Although game balls are standardized, other balls can be useful for training purposes and are perfect for fine-tuning particular skills and techniques.

5. *Lacrosse balls can come in different colors. Source: No machine-readable author provided. Yarnalgo assumed (based on copyright claims)., Public domain, via Wikimedia Commons: https://commons.wikimedia.org/wiki/File:Lax_balls.jpg*

In men's games, the ball is primarily white and sometimes a bright lime green or orange. Women usually use a yellow ball as per lacrosse rules and guidelines. Training balls typically vary in color because it is not as important to meet strict specifications at practice as in a real game. However, practicing with regulation balls is beneficial since your training environment will mimic real game conditions. The balls you use will differ depending on what you want to achieve with your training. For example, heavier, weighted balls improve strength and endurance. Practice balls can also be a little softer than game balls to avoid getting injured before a match.

Lacrosse balls are made from vulcanized rubber. This durable material allows the ball to take endless hits before it is broken or damaged beyond use. Professionals use new balls for every game, but it is common for balls to be reused continuously for budget purposes in amateur leagues. The durable ball has a rubber coating on the outside with a string core also made from rubber. Lacrosse balls have a decent bounce but are not as light as balls used in other sports like tennis. The hardball can injure you if flung directly at you at high speeds. The ball's texture and solidity are why so much safety gear is required. The women's game is not fully impacted like their male counterparts who wear helmets, but they even wear goggles to protect from being blinded by a stick or the ridiculously speedy ball.

Lacrosse balls last for a long time, especially considering the balls are often swapped in the middle of games. The balls can be cheap when bought in bulk, but they cost about $4 on average. Balls that meet regulatory standards are between 62.7 mm and 64.7 mm in size. The size will change according to the league's specific rules or region. Training balls vary more in size than game balls. With continued use, balls become slick and smooth, rendering them unusable, but the durability of lacrosse balls ensures that it is years before this happens. The hardness of the ball is why so much safety equipment is needed, especially for the goalkeeper. Unlike inflatable or hollow balls used in some sports, the lacrosse ball is solid.

# Chapter 4: Lacrosse Positions and Team Play

Lacrosse is a fast-paced, exhilarating sport requiring individual skills and effective teamwork. This chapter explores the techniques and strategies that can help players position themselves and play together cohesively as a team. Whether you're a beginner looking to understand the fundamentals or an experienced player seeking to refine your game, these insights into lacrosse gameplay will help you make the most of your time on the field.

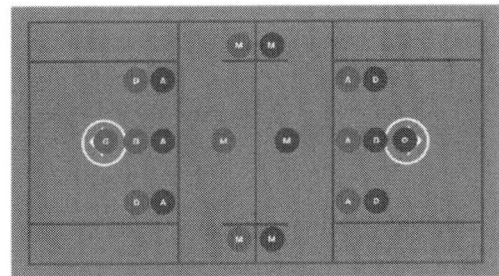

Lacrosse Player Positions

6. *Lacrosse player positions. Source: https://www.rookieroad.com/img/lacrosse/lacrosse-player-positions.png*

You must understand standard practices and strategies for better positioning and team play. Here are some to be familiar with:

## Player Positioning of Attackers

### Cutting

Cutting is a crucial skill for attackers. It involves making precise and timely movements to get open for a pass and create a scoring opportunity. Cutters should read the defense, anticipate passes, and make decisive cuts to open spaces.

### Dodging

Dodging refers to a player's ability to use quick and deceptive moves to bypass defenders. This skill is essential for attackers to navigate through the opposing defense, create shooting lanes, and initiate offensive plays.

### Off-Ball Movement

Off-ball movement is about creating space and providing passing options for teammates. Attackers who move without the ball can confuse defenders, make it challenging for them to cover multiple players, and open up opportunities for their teammates.

## Midfielders Positioning

### Transition Play

Midfielders play a dual role, often transitioning between offense and defense. Effective transition play means knowing when to push the ball up the field on offense and when to drop back and help on defense. Midfielders must be conditioned to run the full length of the field.

**Ground Ball Control**

Ground balls are often contested in lacrosse, and winning possession can be a game-changer. Midfielders must master techniques for scooping ground balls, using the head of their stick and body positioning.

**Defensive Stance**

Even though midfielders have an offensive role, they must also be competent defenders. They must understand when and how to slide to cover offensive players penetrating the defense.

## Defense Positions

**Stance and Footwork**

Defensive players must maintain a low, athletic stance, including keeping their feet shoulder-width apart, knees bent, and stick positioned to block passing and shooting lanes. Proper footwork allows them to stay with attackers and make quick adjustments.

**Stick Checks**

Stick checks are defensive moves that disrupt the opponent's ability to pass, catch, or shoot. The precision and timing of checks are crucial to avoid penalties and effectively dislodge the ball from the offensive player's stick.

**Sliding**

Defensive slides are a fundamental aspect of team defense. When an offensive player beats their defender, a teammate's responsibility is to slide and cover the attacker.

Understanding when to slide and when to stay with their assignment is essential.

**Verbal Communication**

Players must communicate loudly and clearly on the field. They should call out the names of opponents they are marking, alert teammates to open players, and give information about the game situation (e.g., shot clock, time left in a penalty).

**Non-Verbal Communication**

Beyond words, non-verbal communication is essential, including hand signals, body language, and eye contact. Teammates should have a shared understanding of these signals to coordinate effectively.

**Ball Movement**

**Passing**

Accurate and crisp passing is essential to maintain possession and create scoring opportunities. Players need to master various passes, including overhead, sidearm, and bounce passes, while being mindful of defensive pressure.

**Catching**

Cleanly catching the ball is equally important. Players should have soft hands to receive passes, reduce turnovers, and maintain offensive flow.

**Offensive Sets**

Offensive sets are structured formations and movements that help create scoring chances. Players must understand their roles within these sets, whether they are initiators, cutters, or feeders. Recognizing the defense's positioning and making quick decisions within these sets is critical.

# Clears and Rides

## Clears

Clearing is moving the ball from the defensive to the offensive end. Players must be well-versed in clearing strategies, including the positioning of players and passing lanes, to ensure a successful transition from defense to offense.

## Rides

Rides are the opposite of clearing and involve pressuring the opponent's clearing attempts. Effective rides disrupt the opposing team's ability to transition to offense, potentially leading to turnovers.

# Transition Play

## Fast Breaks

These are high-speed, offensive situations when the team gains possession of the ball and quickly transitions to the opponent's end. Players must recognize these opportunities, make fast decisions, and execute to create scoring chances.

## Riding

Riding is a defensive strategy applied in transition. Players coordinate to apply pressure on the clearing team, slowing down their progress and forcing turnovers. Effective riding requires teamwork, communication, and anticipation of the clearing team's actions.

# Special Situations

## Man-Down Defense

It's played when a team is at a disadvantage due to penalties. In this situation, players must adopt specific strategies to minimize scoring opportunities for the opposing team.

## Extra Man Offense

It occurs when a team has a man-up advantage, often due to penalties on the opposing team. Players must capitalize on this advantage by executing structured plays to create scoring opportunities.

Mastering these techniques and strategies is a continuous process requiring practice, teamwork, and a deep understanding of the game. By focusing on these lacrosse aspects, players can elevate their skills and contribute to their team's success on the field.

# Player Positions and Responsibilities

Lacrosse teams typically have three main player positions: Attack, Midfield, and Defense. Each position has distinct roles and responsibilities contributing to the team's overall performance. Here's a detailed breakdown of these positions:

# Attack

Attackers are primarily responsible for generating scoring opportunities and maintaining ball possession on the offensive end of the field. They operate in the offensive zone and are typically positioned near the opposing team's goal.

## Attacker Responsibilities

### Scoring

Attackers are the primary goal scorers. They need strong shooting accuracy and the ability to finish scoring opportunities.

### Feeding

Attackers must be adept at passing and setting up their teammates for goals. They often feed the ball to cutters and midfielders to create offensive plays.

### Ball Retention

Attackers must maintain ball possession and avoid turnovers. They should protect the ball, especially in tight situations, to ensure the team maintains offensive pressure.

### Crease Play

Some attackers specialize in "crease play" and are responsible for creating scoring opportunities around the crease area. They must have excellent stick skills and operate in tight spaces.

# Midfield

Midfielders are versatile players who cover the entire field. They are responsible for offensive and defensive aspects of the game and must have excellent endurance.

## Midfield Responsibilities

### Transition Play

Midfielders are significant in transitioning the ball from the defensive to the offensive end and vice versa. They must be able to run the full length of the field efficiently.

### Offensive Scoring

Midfielders can contribute to the scoring effort and often initiate offensive plays. They need to be accurate shooters and passers.

### Ground Balls

Winning ground balls is a critical responsibility for midfielders. They must use their stick skills and body positioning to secure ground balls and maintain possession.

### Defensive Duties

Midfielders must play strong defense, helping prevent the opposing team from scoring. It includes marking midfielders and occasionally covering opposing attackers.

### Face-Offs

Some midfielders specialize in face-offs, competing for ball control at the center circle at the start of each quarter and after goals. It requires quick reflexes and exceptional stick skills.

## Defense

Defenders protect their team's goal and prevent the opposing team from scoring. They operate in the defensive zone to disrupt offensive plays.

### Defender Responsibilities

### Marking Attackers

Defenders typically mark the opposing team's attackers. They must stay close to their assigned attackers to minimize shooting opportunities.

**Sticks Checks**

Defenders use stick checks to disrupt offensive players' stick handling and passing. These checks must be well-timed to avoid penalties.

**Ground Balls**

Like midfielders, defenders must be adept at winning ground balls to regain possession for their team.

**Slides and Help Defense**

When an offensive player beats their defender, a nearby defender's responsibility is to slide and cover the attacker. Team defense and communication are crucial in sliding effectively.

**Clearing**

Defenders play a role in clearing the ball from the defensive to the offensive end. They must make accurate passes to start offensive possessions.

**Goalie Support**

Defenders should assist the goalie by limiting shooting angles for opponents and clearing rebounds.

Lacrosse is dynamic, and players must adapt to various in-game situations. Versatility, communication, and teamwork are all essential for success in these positions. Additionally, lacrosse players often develop specialized skills and strategies catering to their specific roles on the field, helping them excel in their designated positions and responsibilities.

# The Importance of Teamwork

## Ball Movement and Possession

7. *Teamwork is crucial for maintaining possession of the ball in lacrosse. Source: https://pixabay.com/photos/lacrosse-player-action-stick-1568239/*

Teamwork is crucial for maintaining possession of the ball in lacrosse. Effective ball movement and passing among teammates are central to controlling the game's tempo and setting up offensive plays. Players can advance the ball up the field while maintaining possession when they work together to pass accurately and strategically. This control keeps the opposing team on the defensive and allows more opportunities to set up scoring chances.

Furthermore, teamwork enables players to spread out and position themselves effectively, creating passing lanes and angles that can be exploited to move the ball efficiently. Quick and precise passes are key to preventing turnovers and maintaining offensive pressure.

**Creating Scoring Opportunities**

Lacrosse is a sport where offensive plays are often executed through coordinated teamwork. Teammates work together to create scoring opportunities by setting screens, making off-ball cuts, and creating space for each other. For example, attackers may set picks to free up a teammate, while a midfielder might make a well-timed cut to receive a pass in an advantageous scoring position.

The success of these offensive strategies depends on players understanding their roles within the team and executing them in unison. Effective teamwork in these scenarios leads to more scoring chances and increases the probability of successful conversions.

**Defense and Communication**

Strong teamwork is vital on the defensive end of the field. Communication and cooperation among defensive players are essential for limiting the opposing team's scoring opportunities. Players must work together to defend against quick and agile attackers, often requiring quick switches and slides to cover offensive threats.

Effective communication is a cornerstone of teamwork. Players must verbally communicate their assignments, call out threats, and coordinate defensive strategies in real-time. When a defender gets beaten, a teammate must slide to help cover the attacking player, and this coordinated effort requires trust and collaboration among the defensive unit.

**Transition Play**

Transition plays, involving moving the ball from defense to offense and vice versa, rely heavily on teamwork. Teammates must quickly transition up and down the field, maintaining possession and creating advantageous situations. In offensive transitions, players must work together to exploit gaps in the opposing defense, creating fast-break opportunities.

Defensively, teammates must coordinate their efforts to disrupt the opponent's transition, apply pressure, and limit scoring chances.

Effective teamwork in transition play often leads to goals or prevents the opposing team from capitalizing on fast-break opportunities, making it a critical aspect of a successful lacrosse game.

Undoubtedly, teamwork is the backbone of lacrosse success, extending to aspects like clearing and riding, offensive and defensive strategies, time management, and creating a supportive team atmosphere. The sum of these parts leads to overall success on the field.

# Chapter 5: Ball Control and Passing

In lacrosse, ball control and passing are the bottom-line skills to learn. This chapter is dedicated to mastering ball control and passing techniques and exploring their intricacies. Throughout the upcoming sections, you will explore topics like developing critical ball-handling skills and mastering various passes while understanding the nuances of controlling the ball. Whether you're a newcomer striving to build a solid foundation or a seasoned player seeking to refine your techniques, this chapter aims to provide valuable insights to enhance your ball control and passing skills.

## Developing Essential Ball Handling Skills

These skills include everything from catching and cradling to ground ball pickups and protecting the ball from opponents. Mastering these fundamentals is essential for maintaining possession, moving the ball effectively, and succeeding in offensive and defensive situations. Here's a detailed breakdown of developing essential ball-handling skills:

# Catching the Ball

**Two-Handed Catching**

8. Beginners are often taught to catch the ball using both hands. Source: https://pixabay.com/photos/lacrosse-player-stick-ball-action-1533938/

Beginners are often taught to catch the ball using both hands. This ensures greater control and reduces the chances of dropping the ball. It's crucial to practice catching with both hands to become an all-around player.

## One-Handed Catching

As players progress, they can catch the ball with one hand. This skill is essential for reaching for passes not within immediate reach and maintaining momentum while running.

## Reaction Time

Catching in lacrosse usually involves fast-paced play. Developing quick reflexes and improving reaction time through drills and repetitive practice is vital.

## Cradling

Cradling is the technique used to maintain possession of the ball while moving. It involves rotating the stick back and forth and keeping the ball in the pocket.

## Ball Protection

Cradling helps in ball control and shields the ball from opponents. It's essential to cradle the ball effectively to prevent defenders from checking it out of your stick.

## Variety of Movements

Players should practice cradling while stationary, walking, running, and dodging. It will help in adapting the cradling technique to various in-game scenarios.

## Ground Ball Pickups

Scooping Technique: Picking up ground balls requires precise scooping techniques. Players should use the scoop of their stick head and body positioning to pick up ground balls efficiently.

### Quick Hands

Ground balls are often contested, and having quick hands to secure possession is crucial. Drills to improve hand-eye coordination and speed are invaluable for this aspect.

### Body Protection

Protecting the body while scooping ground balls is vital. Using body positioning to shield the ball from opposing players and avoid body checks is a key skill.

## Passing the Ball

### Accuracy

Accurate passing is essential in lacrosse. Players should practice different passes, including overhead, sidearm, and bounce passes, to ensure precise ball placement.

### Timing

Understanding when to make a pass is as crucial as the accuracy of the pass. Players must develop a sense of timing to make the right pass at the right moment.

### Passing Under Pressure

Drills that simulate game scenarios and apply defensive pressure help players develop the ability to pass effectively in challenging situations.

## Shooting the Ball

### Shooting Technique

Ball-handling skills also extend to shooting. Developing a consistent and effective shooting technique is essential for scoring goals.

### Shooting Accuracy

Like passing, shooting requires accuracy. Players should aim for specific areas of the goal and practice shooting with both hands to become versatile and unpredictable.

### Shooting on the Run

Shooting while on the move is a valuable skill. Practicing shooting on the run and from various angles enhances a player's offensive capabilities.

## Protecting the Ball

### Stick Protection

Players must learn to shield the ball from defenders using their stick, body, and off-hand. This skill prevents turnovers and maintains possession.

### Dodge Moves

Players can protect the ball while evading defenders and creating offensive opportunities using dodge moves, such as split or face dodges.

Developing essential ball-handling skills in lacrosse takes time and consistent practice. Players should focus on improving their skills with both hands, honing their reaction time, and understanding when and how to use each skill effectively in different game situations. This foundation is crucial for success in lacrosse and opens the door to more advanced techniques as players progress in their skill development.

## Mastering Different Types of Passes

Mastering these pass types allows players to adapt to various in-game situations and maintain possession. Here are some of the most common passes in lacrosse:

**Overhead Pass**

The overhead pass is the most basic and widely used in lacrosse. To execute it, stand upright with both hands on the stick, swing the stick overhead, and throw the ball to a teammate using the wrists and arms. This pass is versatile and suitable for short and long distances.

**Sidearm Pass**

*9. The sidearm pass. Source: https://www.rookieroad.com/img/lacrosse/lacrosse-sidearm-pass.png*

A sidearm pass is delivered with a lower arm motion, typically starting at waist level or even lower. This pass is valuable for threading the ball through tight defensive spaces, especially when defenders are close. It's crucial for evading stick checks and making quick, accurate passes.

**Bounce Pass**

A bounce pass is thrown downward toward the ground, causing the ball to bounce before reaching the recipient. This pass effectively avoids defenders' sticks and creates unpredictable ball movement. When executed correctly, the ball can change direction when hitting the ground, making it challenging for defenders to intercept.

**Behind-the-Back Pass**

*10. Behind-the-back pass. Source: https://www.rookieroad.com/img/lacrosse/lacrosse-behind-the-back-pass.png*

The behind-the-back pass is a more advanced and flashy technique. To execute it, cradle the ball behind your back and flick the stick in one fluid motion to pass it to a teammate behind you. This pass can be unpredictable and valuable when a conventional pass is not feasible.

**Feed Pass**

Feed passes are used primarily by attackers and midfielders to set up scoring opportunities. These passes are thrown to a teammate near the goal, allowing a quick shot on the net. Timing and accuracy are essential to deliver the ball to the shooter in the perfect spot for a goal-scoring opportunity.

**Clearing Pass**

Defenders and goalies use clearing passes to transition from defense to offense. These passes require distance and accuracy to move the ball up the field effectively. Clearing passes are vital for breaking out of defensive situations and starting offensive plays.

**Skip Pass**

A skip pass is thrown low and hard across the field to a teammate on the opposite side. This pass is often used to quickly change the point of attack, catching the defense off guard. The low trajectory helps avoid defenders' sticks.

**Behind-the-Cage Pass**

Attackers and players behind the opponent's goal often use behind-the-cage passes. These passes are executed from behind the goal to set up scoring opportunities or maintain ball control. They can change the game's tempo and create opportunities for cutters and shooters.

**Off-Hand Pass**

Proficiency with both hands is a hallmark of a skilled lacrosse player. Developing your off-hand pass is essential for maintaining versatility and unpredictability on the field. Players should practice and improve their off-hand passing to become well-rounded.

**Feeder Pass**

Players use feeder passes primarily focused on creating scoring opportunities for their teammates. They deliver the ball accurately and with perfect timing to a teammate in an advantageous scoring position, setting them up for a successful shot.

**Man-Down Pass**

Quick and accurate ball movement is crucial to breaking down the opposing defense in man-down situations, where a team is a player short due to penalties. Man-down passes are characterized by their speed and precision, helping to exploit defensive weaknesses created by the manpower disadvantage.

**Behind-the-Head Pass**

A behind-the-head pass is executed by flicking the ball behind your head to a teammate. This pass can be particularly effective when a defender's stick or body may block a conventional pass. It's a versatile technique that adds an element of surprise to your passing arsenal.

**Cutting Pass**

Cutting passes are used when a player makes a sharp and often diagonal movement through the defense to receive a pass from a teammate. The success of cutting passes relies on precise timing to connect with the cutting player, allowing them to maintain their momentum and have a clear scoring opportunity.

## Quick-Stick Pass

The quick-stick pass is executed by catching and releasing the ball in a single swift motion. This pass is excellent for rapid ball movement and can catch defenders off guard. It's ideal for close-quarters plays where a quick release is necessary.

Each pass type has its particular purpose and role in lacrosse, and players must practice and master these skills to adapt to different game situations. The ability to execute these passes with precision and confidence enhances a player's overall performance and contributes to successful team play on the lacrosse field.

## Tips to Improve Ball Control and Passing

### For Ball Control

**Master the Cradle**

Spend time perfecting your cradling technique. Practice cradling the ball while walking, running, and dodging. Develop a strong, consistent cradle that protects the ball and maintains control.

**Wall Ball Drills**

Use a wall or rebounder to perform wall ball drills regularly. This drill helps you improve your stick skills, including catching and cradling. Focus on receiving passes cleanly and executing quick cradles.

**Off-Hand Development**

Strengthen your non-dominant hand through dedicated practice. Being proficient with both hands gives you a significant advantage in ball control and passing.

## Ground Ball Drills

Practice ground ball pickups regularly. Work on your scooping technique, using your stick's scoop and body positioning to secure ground balls efficiently.

## Ball Protection

Use your body, stick, and off-hand to shield the ball from defenders. Use your body as a barrier between the ball and your opponent.

## Quick Reaction Training

Improve your hand-eye coordination and reaction time with specific drills. For instance, have a partner throw balls at you and work on catching them quickly.

## Strengthen Your Wrists

Robust wrist control is the basis for ball control and quick cradling. Perform wrist-strengthening exercises to improve your stick-handling abilities.

## Game-Like Situations

Incorporate game scenarios into your practice. Simulate defensive pressure or offensive plays to get accustomed to ball control under realistic conditions.

## Mental Focus

Always stay focused on the ball. Keeping your eye on the ball, especially during catching and cradling, is essential for control.

## Stick Maintenance

Regularly check and repair your lacrosse stick. Ensure the pocket and shooting strings are set up correctly to optimize ball control.

# For Passing

## Work on Fundamental Skills

Start with fundamental skills like catching, cradling, and ground ball pickups. These are prerequisites for effective passing.

## Practice Different Pass Types

Regularly practice various pass types, including overhead, sidearm, bounce, and skip passes. Develop proficiency in executing each type accurately.

## Wall Ball

Wall ball drills are invaluable for passing improvement. Focus on passing the ball accurately and consistently against a wall or rebounder.

## Passing Accuracy

Use targets or designated areas to aim for during your passing drills. Consistently hitting these targets will enhance your passing accuracy.

## Quick Decision-Making

Work on making quick decisions about which pass to use in different game situations. Building lacrosse IQ is essential for effective passing.

## Man-Down and Man-up Scenarios

Practice passing and ball movement during man-down and man-up situations to improve your ability to exploit these opportunities.

**Game-Like Scenarios**

Simulate realistic game scenarios in your practice sessions. Incorporate defensive pressure and specific offensive plays into your passing drills.

**Off-Hand Development**

Focus on developing your off-hand passing skills. Being proficient with both hands makes you a more versatile player.

**Game Vision**

Work on developing a better awareness of the field and your teammates. Understanding where your teammates are and anticipating their movements is essential for effective passing.

**Mental Toughness**

Maintain mental composure during high-pressure situations. Keep a clear focus and make accurate passes even when under defensive pressure.

**Seek Coaching**

Consider working with a lacrosse coach who will give you personalized guidance and constructive feedback on your ball control and passing skills.

Improving ball control and passing takes time and consistent effort. Incorporate these tips into your training routine and focus on continuous practice to enhance these essential lacrosse control and passing skills.

# Chapter 6: Shooting and Scoring

In the game of lacrosse, scoring goals by shooting the ball is where the action happens. This chapter is about getting better at shooting and scoring goals. We'll focus on the basic skills and intelligent moves you need to be a successful goal-scorer. From learning how to shoot correctly to understanding the correct times and places to take a shot, we'll cover all the essential stuff.

*11. The action happens when balls are shot to score goals. Source: https://www.pexels.com/photo/sport-game-competition-net-67870/*

These skills are your pathway to success, from honing your shooting techniques to making shrewd shot choices. Regardless of your expertise level, know that continuous practice and game awareness will be your allies on this journey. Keep striving to improve, and with dedication, you'll evolve into a dependable scorer in lacrosse.

## Shooting and Scoring in Lacrosse

### Grip and Stance

The first step to becoming a proficient scorer in lacrosse is understanding your grip and stance. Your grip on the lacrosse stick is crucial. Your dominant hand should be positioned higher on the stick's shaft, while your non-dominant hand should be closer to the stick's base. This grip provides control and leverage.

Regarding your stance, start with your feet shoulder-width apart. Bend your knees slightly to establish a stable base, and hold the stick with the head near your ear. This position gives you flexibility and control as you prepare to shoot.

### Shooting Mechanics

Practical shooting mechanics are essential for accurate and powerful shots. Although you might have read about these concepts in earlier chapters, here's a quick overview:

**Wrist Snap:** Your wrists play a pivotal role in the accuracy and power of your shot. As you release the ball, focus on snapping your wrists. This snap creates the necessary whip-like motion for a precise and potent shot.

**Follow Through:** After releasing the ball, your stick should continue its movement, pointing in the desired direction. A proper follow-through ensures your shot is on target and maintains control.

## Target Selection

Scoring in lacrosse begins with choosing the right target. Whether aiming for a specific spot in the goal or a vulnerable area the goalie is guarding, pinpoint your target. Visualize where the ball must end and keep your eyes on that spot.

## Shot Types

Master a range of shots to adapt to different game situations. Different shots you can make are explained later in this chapter. Learning these shot types, evaluating the in-game situation, and transitioning from one technique to another can turn the tides in your favor.

## Shot Placement

Scoring hinges on precise shot placement. Familiarize yourself with the goalie's weaknesses and aim for those areas. Corners are often the most challenging spots for goalies to defend. These areas give you the best chance of scoring a goal.

## Timing and Deception

To outwit the goalie, work on your timing and use deception:

**Fakes:** Employ head and body fakes to deceive the goalie and defenders. A well-executed fake can create shooting opportunities when the goalie is off balance.

**Dodges:** Use dodges to create space and get past defenders. When you have a step on a defender, you'll have a better angle for a shot.

### Practice

Regular practice enhances your shooting skills, so work on shooting from different angles, distances, and game situations. Repetition is key to improving your accuracy and effectiveness.

### Game Awareness

Scoring is about individual skill and understanding the broader game context. Be aware of the game situation, including the score, time left, and defensive positioning. Based on these factors, make smart decisions on when to shoot and when to pass.

### Quick Release

Developing a quick release is a valuable asset. A swift release catches the goalie and defenders off guard. To improve your release speed, practice catching and releasing the ball rapidly. Quick, accurate releases make it difficult for the defense to react.

### Mental Toughness

Scoring goals in lacrosse often involves high-pressure situations. Maintain your composure and stay focused when you have scoring opportunities. Confidence and mental toughness are essential for successful scoring.

### Learn from Others

Study experienced players and learn from their techniques and strategies. Observing their gameplay can provide valuable insights and inspiration for your scoring techniques.

You'll increase your chances of becoming a successful lacrosse scorer by honing your shooting mechanics, understanding shot placement, and incorporating fakes and deception into your gameplay.

# Shooting Techniques in Lacrosse

## Overhand Shot

**Lacrosse Overhand Shot**

*12. Overhand shot. Source: https://www.rookieroad.com/img/lacrosse/lacrosse-overhand-shot.png*

The overhand shot is the most common and versatile shooting technique. To execute it, bring your stick above your shoulder, release the ball overhand, and follow through. This technique offers precision and power and is effective for close and long-range shots.

## Sidearm Shot

**Lacrosse Sidearm Shot**

*13. Sidearm shot. Source: https://www.rookieroad.com/img/lacrosse/lacrosse-sidearm-shot.png*

The sidearm shot involves a lower arm motion, with the stick positioned around the waist level. It's useful for quick-release shots and getting the ball past defenders trying to block high shots.

**Underhand Shot**

*14. Underhand shot. Source: https://www.rookieroad.com/img/lacrosse/lacrosse-underhand-shot.png*

The underhand shot is executed by bringing the stick low and shooting from a lower angle. It's particularly effective when you're close to the goal and aiming to shoot underneath the goalie's stick or around their legs.

**Bounce Shot**

A bounce shot is designed to keep the ball low and unpredictable. To execute it, aim for a spot on the ground in front of the goalie, causing the ball to bounce before reaching the net. This shot is challenging for goalies to save.

**Behind-the-Back Shot**

The behind-the-back shot is a flashy and less commonly used technique. It involves shooting the ball by flinging the stick behind your back. It is an effective surprise tactic when you're in a tight situation and defenders least expect it.

## Quick-Stick Shot

The quick-stick shot is catching and releasing the ball swiftly. It's useful in close-quarters situations when you need to make a rapid shot without cradling. A quick stick shot can catch goalies and defenders off guard.

## Dunk Shot

The dunk shot is used when you're very close to the goal. It is dunking the ball into the net by pushing it in with your stick. It's effective for point-blank shots.

## Time and Room Shot

A time and room shot is taken with plenty of space and time to wind up and release the ball with maximum power and accuracy. These shots are often taken from a distance and require a full wind-up to generate velocity.

## Backhand Shot

The backhand shot is executed by shooting the ball with the back of your stick. This technique is advantageous when you're in a position where a conventional shot is challenging.

## Change-up Shot

A change-up shot involves altering the speed and trajectory of your shot to confuse the goalie. Varying your shots with different speeds and release points is highly effective.

## Placement Shot

Rather than focusing on the power of your shot, placement shots emphasize accuracy. These are carefully aimed shots, often targeting the goal's corners, where goalies have a harder time making saves.

**Dive Shot**

A dive shot is when you're airborne and extend your body toward the goal, releasing the ball while in the air. It's a dramatic and athletic shot often seen when players dive across the crease.

Knowing when to use each technique and adapting to different game situations will make you a versatile and effective offensive player.

## Strategies for Scoring Goals

**Off-Ball Movement**

Effective off-ball movement is the foundation of lacrosse offense. Players should constantly be on the move, cutting through open spaces and setting up positions, making them available for passes. Movement can confuse defenders and create opportunities for the ball carrier and off-ball players.

**Feeding and Assisting**

Lacrosse is a team sport, and successful scorers aren't solely focused on their own goals. Assisting teammates is just as important. Accurate passing and setting up your teammates with scoring opportunities are key to the offensive strategy. Look for open teammates and deliver precise passes to set up easy goals.

**Pick and Roll**

The pick and roll is a well-known offensive tactic. It involves one player setting a pick (a blocking screen) for a teammate who possesses the ball. The ball carrier uses the pick to gain an advantage over their defender and create a scoring opportunity. Timing, communication, and execution are crucial for a successful pick and roll.

**Draw and Dump**

The draw-and-dump strategy involves a player drawing the defense's attention with the ball, typically achieved through dodging toward the goal. Once the defense collapses on the ball carrier, they "dump" the ball to an open teammate, creating a scoring opportunity as the defense is out of position.

**Transition Play**

Fast breaks and transition plays occur when your team gains possession and rapidly moves the ball up the field. Transition plays capitalize on the disarray of the opposing defense, often leading to high-percentage scoring opportunities.

**Creating Mismatches**

A significant aspect of offensive strategy is recognizing and exploiting defensive mismatches. If you're being defended by a slower player or a mismatch in size or skill, use your agility and speed to your advantage.

**Two-Man Game**

The two-man game combines elements of pick and rolls with quick passes between two players. This coordinated approach confuses defenders and creates opportunities for open shooting lanes and passing options.

**Change of Speed and Direction**

Use changes in speed and direction to confound defenders. Quick accelerations and direction changes can help you separate from your defender, creating scoring opportunities as you gain space and time.

**Shot Selection**

Shot selection is a critical part of scoring goals. Be patient and deliberate in choosing when to take a shot. Avoid low-percentage attempts from unfavorable angles likely to be saved by the goalie. Opt for high-percentage shots that maximize your scoring chances.

**Offensive Sets and Plays**

Many lacrosse teams use specific offensive sets and plays. These involve coordinated movements, passes, and screens that aim to confuse the defense and generate open shooting opportunities. A deep understanding of these plays is essential for success.

**Rebounds and Loose Balls**

Scoring often involves capitalizing on rebounds and loose balls around the crease. Quick reflexes, hustle, and proper positioning are vital in these situations. Be ready to scoop up the ball and take a quick shot when it's loose in front of the net.

**Shot Fakes and Deception**

Incorporating shot fakes and deception into your offensive strategy are powerful tools. A well-executed fake can freeze the goalie or defenders, creating a valuable split-second opening for a shot.

**Man-Up (Extra Player) Situations**

Take the numerical advantage when your team has an extra player due to penalties (man-up situation). Work the ball around the offensive zone to exploit defensive gaps, create open shots, and maximize the scoring potential.

## Game Situation Awareness

Being aware of the game situation is crucial for making the right decisions. Consider the score, time remaining, and the situation's urgency, and adjust your strategy accordingly. Sometimes, taking calculated risks is necessary to secure a goal. At other times, maintaining possession and running down the clock is the better choice.

Lacrosse is a physically demanding sport. Building endurance and conditioning is vital for maintaining a high level of play throughout the game. Scoring opportunities often arise late in the game when opponents are tired. Being physically prepared to seize these chances is essential. Incorporating these detailed scoring strategies into your game can make you a more effective and dynamic lacrosse player. By understanding the intricacies of offensive movements and decision-making, you can consistently contribute to your team's success in scoring goals.

# Chapter 7: Lacrosse Defense

Mostly, people only pay a lot of attention to the players who score goals with fancy moves in lacrosse. But there's another important player on the team, the defender. Playing defense in lacrosse is a mix of skills, strategy, and being quick. It's not only about stopping the other team from scoring. It's about being smart and agile. This chapter explains information you should know to be a good defender. Besides coordinating with teammates and using your body effectively, great defense requires defenders to know different tactics and strategies for defense. These tactics and goalie techniques are covered in this chapter. You'll understand how to play good defensive lacrosse when you finish reading.

15. Defenders need to be skilled and quick. Source: Act96, CC BY-SA 4.0 <https://creativecommons.org/licenses/by-sa/4.0>, via Wikimedia Commons: https://commons.wikimedia.org/wiki/File:Men%27s_Lacrosse_Player.jpg

## Key Principles in Defense

### Positioning and Footwork

The foundation of effective defense lies in your stance. Maintain a low, balanced posture, staying nimble to react swiftly to your opponent's moves.

### Stick Position

Your stick should be poised, parallel to the ground, blocking passing lanes and potential shots. The correct stick positioning is critical for intercepting or deflecting the ball.

## Reading the Game

Anticipate your opponent's actions by watching their body language and ball movement closely. This ability to read the game allows you to make well-timed interceptions or blocks.

## Stick Checks

Mastery of various stick checks, including the poke check, lift check, and slap check, is crucial for dislodging the ball from your opponent's possession.

## Body Checks

Use your body to obstruct and impede your opponent's progress within the rules' boundaries. Position yourself effectively to deter them from advancing.

## Teamwork and Communication

Lacrosse is a team sport, and cohesive defense hinges on effective collaboration. Employ slide defense to support teammates in need and sustain open lines of communication to ensure everyone is on the same page.

## Ground Ball Mastery

Swift and precise ground ball pickups are non-negotiable. Scoop the ball with dexterity and shield it with your body to retain possession.

## Adapting to Special Situations

Be prepared for exceptional scenarios like man-down defense or clearing the ball from your defensive zone. Adapt your strategies accordingly to meet the specific demands of the moment.

### Continuous Growth

Commit to regular practice sessions to sharpen your defensive skills. Seek inspiration and learn from professional games, integrating their techniques into your play.

## Defensive Tactics and Strategies

### Individual Defensive Tactics

- **Body Positioning:** This tactic involves keeping a low and balanced stance to stay between your opponent and the goal. Effectively positioning yourself makes it challenging for attackers to drive past you and take high-percentage shots.

- **Stick Positioning**: Keep your stick up and parallel to the ground to block passing lanes and shots. Proper stick positioning is crucial for intercepting passes and deflecting shots.

- **Stick Checks:** Stick checks are defensive moves using your stick to disrupt the ball carrier's stickhandling, passing, or shooting. Examples include the poke check, lift check, and slap check.

- **Footwork:** Quick and agile footwork is essential for staying with your opponent, shadowing their movements, and responding rapidly to their actions.

### Team Defensive Tactics

- **Man-to-Man Defense:** In this tactic, specific defenders are assigned to mark individual attackers. It ensures close coverage and limits opponents' scoring opportunities by continuous pressure on their assigned players.

- **Zone Defense:** Zone defense is about defenders guarding specific areas of the field rather than marking individual players. Defenders focus on areas like the crease and high-scoring zones to deny attackers easy access to these prime-scoring locations.

- **Sliding and Double-Teaming:** When an attacker beats their defender and drives toward the goal, a nearby teammate slides over to double-team the attacker. This added pressure disrupts the attack and forces the attacker into making rushed decisions.

- **Communication:** Effective defense requires constant communication among teammates to coordinate defensive efforts, call out picks, and alert each other to opponents' movements.

## Defensive Strategies

**Pressuring and Forcing Turnovers**

- **Ball Pressure**: Applying pressure on the ball carrier disrupts their ability to pass or dodge effectively. It's a fundamental strategy to obstruct the opponent's offense.

- **Forcing Bad Shots:** Position yourself strategically to force the ball carrier into taking low-percentage shots. This tactic increases the chances of your goalkeeper making saves.

- **Checking and Stick Checks**: Use stick checks, like the poke check, to dislodge the ball from the opponent's stick and force turnovers.

## Riding

Riding is an offensive-oriented strategy where your team applies pressure on the clearing players from the opposing team to disrupt their transition into the offensive zone. Effective riding can lead to turnovers and regaining possession.

## Clearing and Transition Defense

Clearing involves efficiently moving the ball out of the defensive zone when your team gains possession and transitioning into offense. Transition defense focuses on quickly adjusting from offense to defense to prevent fast breaks and limit scoring opportunities when the opposing team gets possession.

## Ground Ball Battles

Engaging in ground ball contests is a key strategy to secure possession for your team. It entails scooping ground balls efficiently and protecting them from opponents' checks.

## Penalty Killing (Man-Down Defense)

Penalty killing is a specialized strategy for when your team is a player down due to penalties. It includes effective defensive tactics, like zone defense, shot blocking, and coordinated efforts to minimize the opponent's scoring chances during man-down situations.

## Adapting to Opponent's Style

Analyzing your opponent's offensive strategies and adapting your defense accordingly is a strategic approach.

Understanding their tendencies allows you to anticipate their moves and make timely adjustments.

**Maintaining Composure and Discipline**

Playing with discipline is essential to avoid unnecessary penalties. Defensive aggression must be legal, ensuring you maintain a strong defense without giving the opposing team man-up opportunities.

**Patient Sliding**

Patient sliding is a strategic approach in sliding defense, where defenders resist sliding too early. This tactic allows the on-ball defender to apply pressure effectively before the slide arrives, minimizing open passing lanes and shooting opportunities.

When applied effectively, these defensive tactics and strategies form a robust foundation for a successful defense. They create a dynamic and adaptable defense that can stifle the opponent's offensive efforts and secure your team's competitiveness.

## Goalie Techniques

**Positioning**

Goalie positioning is fundamental to success. They stand with their feet shoulder-width apart, knees slightly bent, and weight forward on the balls of their feet. This stance helps them react in any direction quickly. Their upper body remains upright, with shoulders square to the shooter. This square positioning maximizes the coverage of the goal, making it more challenging for shooters to find open angles.

## Shot Stopping

Goalies must master the art of shot-stopping. This skill involves several components, including hand-eye coordination, quick reflexes, and an innate ability to anticipate where the shot is headed. By reading the shooter's body language, goalies can better predict the shot's trajectory. They use their stick, body, or feet to make saves. The stick intercepts shots, while the body serves as a last-resort barrier, and the feet are employed for low shots.

## Clearing

Clearing is a critical component of a goalie's role. After making a save, the goalie must efficiently clear the ball to a teammate or initiate a fast break for the team. This demands quick decision-making, field awareness, and precise passing. Goalies must evaluate their options, decide whether to pass or carry the ball, and execute the chosen action swiftly.

## Outlet Passing

Outlet passing is a core skill for goalies. To initiate offensive transitions or clears, goalies use a split grip on their stick, with one hand positioned near the head for making quick passes and the other on the stick's throat for control. This split grip offers a balance of accuracy and control. Goalies must be proficient at making accurate, on-target passes to their teammates to maintain possession or start offensive opportunities.

## Angle Play

Understanding and applying angles is crucial for goalies. They aim to reduce the shooter's angle to the goal, making the net appear smaller from the shooter's perspective. Based on the shooter's location and angle of approach, the goalie must adjust their position. By limiting the visible net, goalies increase their chances of making saves.

### Footwork

Quick and precise footwork is an essential aspect of a goalie's skill set. Goalies must be agile to move laterally and adjust their positioning in response to the ball and the offensive players' movements. Proper footwork allows goalies to maintain an optimal stance and react efficiently to different shooting scenarios.

### Hand Positioning

Hand positioning on the stick is a critical component of making saves. Goalies typically use a split grip, with one hand near the head for making saves and the other on the throat of the stick for control. This grip allows goalies to maximize their range and reach while maintaining control of the stick.

### Communication

Effective communication is paramount for goalies. They are the eyes and vocal leaders of the defense. Goalies must maintain constant communication with their defenders, providing direction, calling out slides, and keeping everyone informed about the game's dynamics. This open line of communication helps ensure a well-coordinated defense.

## Goalie Roles

### Shot Stopping

The primary and most fundamental role of a lacrosse goalie is to stop shots and prevent the opposing team from scoring goals. Goalies must be prepared to face shots from various angles, distances, and trajectories. Making saves is their top priority.

## Clearing and Ball Handling

Goalies are pivotal in clearing the ball from the defensive zone and initiating offensive possessions. Their decisions and execution in clearing directly impact the team's transition from defense to offense effectively.

## Quarterback of the Defense

Goalies assume the role of the quarterback of the defense. They are responsible for directing the defenders, recognizing the opponent's strategies, and making real-time adjustments to the defense. They provide guidance on when to slide, how to cover cutters, and overall defensive organization.

## Leadership and Communication

Goalies are vocal leaders on the field. They lead by example, motivate their teammates, and provide crucial information. Effective communication is vital for keeping the defense organized, executing strategies, and making quick, collective decisions.

## Mental Toughness

Goalies often face high-pressure situations, like one-on-one shots or critical moments in a game. Mental toughness is essential for maintaining composure, focus, and resilience during these high-stress periods. Goalies must maintain confidence in their abilities, even in challenging moments.

## Clearing and Transition Play

A successful clear can lead to fast breaks and scoring opportunities for the offensive unit. Goalies must make quick, accurate decisions about clearing the ball to start offensive possessions.

## Stopping Shots from All Angles

Lacrosse goalies must be prepared to stop shots from various angles and distances. They must continually adjust their positioning to track the ball and respond effectively to different shots, whether they are close-range, long-range, or from acute angles.

Lacrosse goalies play a multifaceted role, mastering a range of techniques and assuming leadership and communication responsibilities. Their ability to make crucial saves, clear the ball, and quarterback the defense is central to their team's success.

# Chapter 8: Improving Your Game and Lacrosse Community

Armed with knowledge of the game, you can enter the field and start playing. Over time, you will move from the beginner level to the intermediate. However, playing the game regularly without practicing new skills or adding more drills to your routine will only take you so far. You must keep improving your game to rise through the levels at a steady pace and, at the same time, enjoy every moment of the sport.

*16. Regularly practicing lacrosse can help you improve your skills. Source: https://pixabay.com/photos/lacrosse-lax-player-lacrosse-player-1471740/*

This chapter will take you through the drills and exercises to improve your game in leaps and bounds, and the expert tips included will ensure you surprise your opponents at every step. Then, you will be led to the fantastic world of lacrosse communities, their role in improving your game, and how to find and join them.

## Drills and Exercises for Skill Improvement

You unknowingly practice many drills when you play a lacrosse game, but there are many other valuable skills you don't use even once. It entirely depends on the nature of the game and your strategies. Why not make yourself ready to use every skill? The following drills will provide a healthy push to your game:

**Lacrosse Drills**

- **Cradle:** The action of cradling a lacrosse ball is similar to cradling a child in your arms. It helps you move around the field easily and quickly while holding the ball in the stick's pocket. Running around with the ball without cradling will cause it to fall off or get knocked out by an opponent. A simple drill to improve your cradling is to stand straight with your back touching a wall, hold the stick vertically, and quickly start cradling the ball. Make sure your stick brushes the wall when you cradle each side.

- **Switch Hands:** As you may know, there's no backhand in lacrosse since the ball can be caught in only one side of the pocket. If you hold the stick in your right hand, you will have to switch it to your left hand to catch a ball coming from your left side.

To practice switching hands quickly, throw the ball at the wall with your right hand and switch the stick to your left hand to catch it. Then, throw the ball with your left and catch it with your right. Practice this drill for around 10 minutes.

- **Ground Ball Scoop:** Scooping the ball quickly from the ground is an important skill. A split-second difference can mean your opponent gets the ball. Throw an underarm low ball at the wall so it ricochets, rolling on the ground, and scoop it up with your right hand and release it again. The second time, switch hands to scoop it up with your left. Practice this drill for around 10 minutes.

- **Shooting:** While you can shoot the ball in the goal any way you please, the most common form of shooting is an overarm release. It's easier to aim and throw it in with great force. Mark a foot-wide target on the wall and shoot at it from a sufficient distance, around four to five yards, so you can readily dodge the bounce back. Scoop it up and shoot again from a further distance.

- **Passing and Catching:** Passing in lacrosse is more about catching than the accuracy of the throw. Your teammate can pass the ball from any angle, so you must think on your feet to catch the ball. Run along the length of the wall, a yard or two apart. Throw the ball at different angles to the wall and catch it each time it ricochets.

## Lacrosse Exercises

Your proficiency is heavily dependent on your agility and reflexes. Lacrosse may be a contact game, but it's the lithe, athletic players that own the field rather than hulky, muscular ones. The drills will take care of your upper body skills. Your exercises should focus on your lower body.

- **Squats:** Squats are a given for building your lower body. They target your thighs and glutes like no other exercise, and as a bonus, they strengthen your core, a crucial requirement for throwing a powerful shot. Start with weightless squats for a week, two sets of 10-20 reps. Proceed to weighted back squats for a few weeks, followed by front squats, and so on.

- **Lunges:** Another lower body essential is the lunge exercise. They work out your glutes and hamstrings and part of your quadriceps and calves. This exercise's most important benefit for your lacrosse game is improving your balance. If your balance is weak, you cannot hold the lunge position for long, much less bend the back knee. Directly start with weighted lunges suited to your strength. Hold the dumbbells to the sides and perform two sets of 10 reps, increasing sets as you go.

- **Deadlifts:** This is another great exercise to strengthen your core, hamstrings, and glutes, and your back muscles, too. You need to twist and turn a lot during the game, for which back muscles are key. Hold the barbell near your shins with your back straight. Come up and maintain the straight posture, then go down again. If you have access to a hex bar or trap bar, all the better.

- **Box Jumps:** You don't have access to any equipment whatsoever? Practice increased reps and sets of weightless squats and lunges. Box jumps are an excellent addition to your workout routine. Apart from targeting your lower body, it also focuses on your upper body, making you more agile. Find a raised, even platform as high as your knees, and jump on and off simultaneously with both feet.

- **Jump Rope:** A jump rope is the perfect exercise to build overall agility and improve your lacrosse footwork. If you have never done this exercise before, start jumping without a rope. Slowly ease the rope into your workout to improve your footwork.

## Tips for Improving Your Game

Drills and exercises can prepare you for the game and even improve it to a substantial degree. However, you won't reach your true potential unless you play with other players. Your opponents may already be experienced on the field, so observe their game while playing. Here are a few handy tips to surprise your opponents as a beginner:

- Fake your shots. You have already practiced cradling the ball. Put it to good use on the field. When you are in the opponent's defensive area, fake your shots. Act as if you are going to shoot, but at the last moment, cradle the ball and move forward when the defender tries to block your feet.

- Don't look at the ground when you possess the ball. Always hold your stick vertically, cradle the ball often so you don't accidentally drop it, and keep your eyes up. With your stick up, the opponents will feel you are about to pass the ball, making them converge on other players instead of you, possibly leaving you with a clear field to sprint ahead.

- Communicate often during the game. Are you in a good scoring position? Call out for the ball. Is an opponent sneaking up on your teammate? Warn them out loud. Are you faking a pass? Shout the name of the person you will actually be passing it to. Lacrosse is about teamwork, and without proper communication, even a team with the finest players falls apart.

## Joining a Lacrosse Community

*17. A lacrosse community can help you develop your skills. Source: https://pixabay.com/photos/lacrosse-lax-team-players-sport-1501851/*

You can practice drills and moves on your own as long as you have all the right equipment and a wall. You can even play a game with your friends and colleagues if you have access to a ground. But the joy of playing lacrosse with other like-minded players is something else altogether. To experience this joy, join a community.

- A community helps you stay in perfect physical and mental shape for competitive games. Performing drills is boring work, and you may lose interest after a while. On the other hand, playing with a group of like-minded enthusiasts helps you enjoy the game while maintaining your fitness.
- Teamwork is one of the most critical aspects of the game. The only way to get better at it is by playing in a community.
- Players with various skills are a part of the community. If you are lucky, your local community will include national players. You can learn a great deal from them and improve your game rapidly. You can also teach those new to the sport, strengthening your fundamentals.

## Finding a Local Community

Lacrosse communities are found in many parts of the United States. After all, the game was started by the indigenous tribes, so the country is the epicenter of all things lacrosse. Find a community near you by searching for "lacrosse community near me" on Google. For instance, if you reside in Atlanta, Georgia, several results will turn up, including the Atlanta Lacrosse League and the Box Lacrosse Association.

Social media is another good way of finding communities. Many lacrosse groups on Facebook meet regularly on local playing fields. Once you find the right community, reach out to the authorities and ask if you can join. They usually admit players of all levels, including novices.

Is there a tournament in your neighborhood? Watch the games and approach the team managers of your skill level for tryouts. An easier way to get in touch with the managers is to volunteer to help organize the event.

Lacrosse is a physically demanding sport, so keeping your body at its peak fitness is essential. Practicing drills and exercises every day will keep you in top form for game day. Some of the best lifelong friendships are made on the lacrosse field.

# Conclusion

Whether you're a beginner or have some experience, understanding the power of concentration can make a huge difference in your game. In lacrosse, where the action never stops, your focus is the most essential skill necessary. Instead of fixating on winning or losing, concentrate on what you can control – your performance. Think about giving it your all and let everything else follow naturally.

Concentration means being fully present, not dwelling on what happened earlier or worrying about what's next. It's about being in sync with the flow of the game and staying connected to what's happening on the field.

However, you can't force concentration. Trying too hard to focus can backfire, especially when things aren't going your way. Overthinking, forcing plays, and getting tense are common pitfalls. When you're playing at your best, you're not overthinking. You're just doing what feels right.

Positive thinking is another key. Instead of worrying about what you don't want to do, focus on what you want to achieve. Positive thoughts steer your mind in the right direction. They help you stay relaxed and perform at your best.

During a noisy lacrosse game, blocking out distractions is a game-changer. You need total concentration to stay sharp throughout the match. Every play, every one-on-one encounter, must be seen as important. You can't afford to lose focus, so train your mind to stay on track.

In lacrosse, as in life, success often comes down to focus, positivity, and unwavering concentration. It's a sport demanding your best effort and complete dedication to the present moment. As you start your journey, remember that the power to perform is in your hands. So, stay focused, think positively, and tune out distractions. In the exhilarating lacrosse world, the sky's the limit for those who master the art of focused performance. Best of luck and enjoy the thrilling world of lacrosse.

Please leave a review to encourage and inspire other beginners to embark on their lacrosse journey.

# References

(N.d.). Everettlacrosseclub.org. https://www.everettlacrosseclub.org/lax101

(N.d.). Jrminutemenlax.net. https://www.jrminutemenlax.net/page/show/51073-more-lacrosse-drills

(N.d.). Jrminutemenlax.net. https://www.jrminutemenlax.net/page/show/51077-27-tips-for-defensemen

(N.d.). Jrminutemenlax.net. https://www.jrminutemenlax.net/page/show/51073-more-lacrosse-drills

Basic rules of lacrosse. (n.d.). SportsEngine. https://www.sportsengine.com/lacrosse/lacrosses-basic-rules

Brian. (2023, August 17). Elevating your defensive skills in lacrosse: Techniques and tips. STXZ | Private Lacrosse Training. https://stxzlacrosse.com/elevating-your-defensive-skills-in-lacrosse-techniques-and-tips/

CitySide Lacrosse. (n.d.). Citysidelax.com. https://www.citysidelax.com/news-posts/get-in-the-game-discovering-the-benefits-of-joining-a-local-lacrosse-team

Creating success in the game of lacrosse. (n.d.). Cal Ripken Sr. Foundation. https://www.ripkenfoundation.org/blog/creating-success-game-lacrosse

Damon, C. (2016, June 13). The basics of lacrosse team defense: Man on man. Lax Goalie Rat. https://laxgoalierat.com/lacrosse-team-defense/

Damon, C. (n.d.). Twelve ways to destroy a lacrosse goalie's development. SportsEngine. https://www.sportsengine.com/article/lacrosse/twelve-ways-destroy-lacrosse-goalies-development

Edwards, C. (2018, February 25). My top ten lacrosse goalie tips - part 1. Lacrossegoalieuniversity.com. https://lacrossegoalieuniversity.com/top-ten-lacrosse-goalie-tips/

Equipment. (n.d.). USA Lacrosse. https://www.usalacrosse.com/equipment

How to shoot A lacrosse ball. (n.d.). Signature Lacrosse. https://signaturelacrosse.com/blogs/news/how-to-shoot-a-lacrosse-ball

jakenathan. (2020, March 25). 10 easy ways to improve your lacrosse game. Laxweekly.com. https://laxweekly.com/10-ways-improve-lacrosse/

Kamosa, A. (n.d.). Men's lacrosse focuses on teamwork. Stevenson Villager. https://stevensonvillager.com/2603/sports/mens-lacrosse-focuses-on-teamwork/

L., H. (2019, December 16). Lacrosse stick length guide & size chart. Lacrossemonkey.com. https://www.lacrossemonkey.com/learn/lacrosse-stick-length-size-chart

L., H. (2020, February 26). Lacrosse shaft buying guide: Weights, materials & shapes! Lacrossemonkey.com. https://www.lacrossemonkey.com/learn/lacrosse-shaft-weight-buying-guide

L., H. (2020, February 26). Lacrosse shaft buying guide: Weights, materials & shapes! Lacrossemonkey.com. https://www.lacrossemonkey.com/learn/lacrosse-shaft-weight-buying-guide

Lacrosse ball color reasons uses, & options. (n.d.). Signature Lacrosse. https://signaturelacrosse.com/blogs/news/colored-lacrosse-balls

Lacrosse Monkey. (2022, April 12). Lacrosse shot guide: How to shoot a lacrosse ball. Lacrossemonkey.com. https://www.lacrossemonkey.com/learn/how-to-shoot-a-lacrosse-ball

Lacrosse Monkey. (2023, August 18). Types of lacrosse sticks: A complete guide. Lacrossemonkey.com. https://www.lacrossemonkey.com/learn/lacrosse-stick-types

Lacrosse Monkey. (2023, March 21). How to play lacrosse: A 101 guide to lacrosse fundamentals. Lacrossemonkey.com. https://www.lacrossemonkey.com/learn/how-to-play-lacrosse-fundamentals

Lacrosse stationary passing. (n.d.). Kbandstraining.com. https://kbandstraining.com/lacrosse-stationary-passing/

Lacrosse. (2022, December 29). Turf Tank. https://turftank.com/us/academy/rules-of-lacrosse/

Lacrosse. (2022, December 29). Turf Tank. https://turftank.com/us/academy/rules-of-lacrosse/

Lacrosse: Positions of midfielder, attacker, goalie, and defenseman. (n.d.). Ducksters.com. https://www.ducksters.com/sports/lacrossepositions.php

Lacrosse. (2023, June 25). Understanding lacrosse scoring. Medium. https://medium.com/@lacrossee/understanding-lacrosse-scoring-a856d83e3e39

Learning teamwork and sportsmanship with lacrosse. (n.d.). Merakey. https://www.merakey.org/about/news/learning-teamwork-and-sportsmanship-with-lacrosse

Molly. (2022, December 7). 5 lacrosse exercises every player should do. TrainHeroic. https://www.trainheroic.com/blog/5-exercises-for-lacrosse-players/

No title. (n.d.). Prked.com. https://prked.com/blog/What-is-the-best-way-to-practice-passing-a-lacrosse-ball

Reding, T. (2023, February 23). What are the Differences Between Lacrosse Sticks? Sportdecals. https://www.sportdecals.com/blogs/p/what-are-the-differences-between-lacrosse-sticks

Rode, M. (2017, April 29). Lacrosse stick parts - the ultimate guide. Stringers Society Lacrosse. https://stringerssociety.com/blog/parts-of-a-lacrosse-stick/

Rode, M. (2022, December 15). Lacrosse equipment list. Stringers Society Lacrosse. https://stringerssociety.com/blog/lacrosse-equipment-list/

Rookie Road. (2020, February 11). Lacrosse pass types. Rookieroad.com; Rookie Road. https://www.rookieroad.com/lacrosse/pass-types-1742771/

Rookie Road. (2020, February 27). Types of Lacrosse Sticks. Rookieroad.com; Rookie Road. https://www.rookieroad.com/lacrosse/types-of-lacrosse-sticks/

Rookie Road. (2020, February 8). Lacrosse basics. Rookieroad.com; Rookie Road. https://www.rookieroad.com/lacrosse/basics/

Rookie Road. (2021, July 15). Lacrosse balls. Rookieroad.com; Rookie Road. https://www.rookieroad.com/lacrosse/balls/

Simmons, T. (2019, December 19). Lacrosse positions - attack, midfield, Defense, goalie. Elevate Sports; Elevate Sports.

https://www.elevatesportsequipment.com/blogs/news/lacrosse-positions-attack-midfield-defense-goalie

Stick handling and ground balls. (n.d.). Human Kinetics. https://us.humankinetics.com/blogs/excerpt/stick-handling-and-ground-balls

The top gear every lacrosse player needs. (n.d.). Source for Sports. https://www.sourceforsports.ca/blogs/lacrosse/the-top-gear-every-lacrosse-player-needs

What lacrosse stick should I get? (2021, August 16). Gilbert Knights Lacrosse. https://gilbertknightslacrosse.com/2021/08/what-lacrosse-stick-should-i-get/

Wiegand, C. (2017, March 9). Lacrosse tips: How to create different shots. PRO TIPS by DICK'S Sporting Goods; DICK'S Sporting Goods. https://protips.dickssportinggoods.com/sports-and-activities/lacrosse/lacrosse-tips-create-different-shots

Wilson, C. (2019, January 23). How to become A dominant lacrosse defenseman. Lacrosse All Stars. https://laxallstars.com/how-to-become-a-dominant-lacrosse-defenseman/

Zabor, R. (n.d.). From beginner to pro - when to upgrade your lacrosse stick. SportsEngine. https://www.sportsengine.com/article/lacrosse/beginner-pro-when-upgrade-your-lacrosse-stick

Made in the USA
Columbia, SC
01 May 2025